CLIPPINGS

Andrews and McMeel
A Universal Press Syndicate Company
Kansas City

Garden Clippings copyright © 1991 by Smallwood and Stewart, Inc. All rights reserved. Printed in Singapore. No part of this book may be used or reproduced in any manner whatsoever without written permission except in the case of reprints in context of reviews. For information, write Andrews and McMeel, a Universal Press Syndicate Company, 4900 Main Street, Kansas City, Missouri 64112.

Library of Congress Cataloging-in-Publication Data

Garden clippings : a literary bouquet.—1st U.S. ed.
    p.   cm.
  "A Smallwood & Stewart book."
  ISBN 0-8362-7987-5 : $15.00
  1. Gardens.   2. Gardening.   3. Gardens—Quotations, maxims, etc.
4. Gardening—Quotations, maxims, etc.   5. Gardens—Pictorial
Works.   6. Plants, Ornamental—Pictorial works.
  SB455.G35   1991
  635—dc20   91-20662
                                                                      CIP

Designed by Dirk Kaufman
Produced by Smallwood and Stewart, Inc.
New York City

Printed in Singapore
First U.S. edition
1   2   3   4   5   6   7   8   9   10

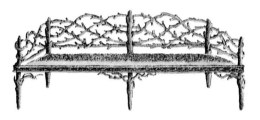

INTRODUCTION

Ever since Man reluctantly left Eden we have sought to create our own versions of that earthly paradise. In fact, the very word "paradise" is derived from the name given to the great enclosed parks enjoyed by the Persian kings. Our Edens have taken many forms, from intricate medieval knot gardens to billowing cottage borders, from the imperious avenues of Versailles to the meticulous arrangements in moss and stones in a Japanese garden.

Places of pleasure, sources of sustenance, gardens—and our love of all that they contain—have nourished a literature that is as diverse and timeless as its subject. Gardeners, of course, have always written passionately about their vocation. The books and essays of the most famous, including Gertrude Jekyll, Louise Beebe Wilder, Russell Page, and Elizabeth Lawrence, are full of insight and wisdom, as well as accounts of the tribulations and trials, and great surprises and pleasures that are essential parts of gardening.

The writings of the great plant hunters such as Robert Fortune and F. Kingdon-Ward, in pursuit of rare specimens on the islands of Japan or in the mountains of Tibet, can be as colorful and as thrilling as any popular fiction. In their works, we find the single-minded zeal of the collector combined with great daring and courage in the searches for plants that are now a familiar part of many garden beds and borders.

Traditionally tokens of gratitude, celebration, and devotion, flowers have probably inspired more verse than any subject save love itself. Flowers figure prominently as symbols in the myths of ancient Greece and in the works of virtually every significant poet since. The Victorians popularized an elaborate symbolism for them, appropriately florid in tone, through which they could coyly pursue their courtships and romances without offense.

According to Gertrude Jekyll, the one lesson she learned from gardening and most wished to pass on to others was the "enduring happiness that the love of a garden gives." Like the lively mix of antique and new, humble and grand flowers in a cottage border, here is a collection of expressions of that inexhaustible pleasure the garden brings.

Lux umbram monstrat, mysteria autem veritas.

Light shows shadow, but truth shows mysteries.

FRENCH SUNDIAL INSCRIPTION

Let others tell of rain and showers;

I only count the shining hours.

ENGLISH SUNDIAL INSCRIPTION

Lux umbra Dei

Light is the shadow of God

ENGLISH SUNDIAL INSCRIPTION

And Winter slumbering in the open air

Wears on her smiling face a dream of Spring.

ANONYMOUS

DAFFODILS

that come before the swallow dares,

And take the winds of March with beauty; . . .

WILLIAM SHAKESPEARE

A Winter's Tale

*S*owing: around 300 pots Poppies—60 Sweet pea—around 60 pots white Agremony — 30 yellow Agremony — Blue sage — Blue Water-lilies in beds greenhouse—Dahlias—Iris Kaempferi.—From the 15th to the 25th, lay the dahlias down to root; plant out those with shoots before I get back.—Don't forget the lily bulbs.—Should the Japanese paeonies arrive plant them immediately if weather permits, taking care initially to protect buds from the cold, as much as from the heat of the sun. Get down to pruning: rose trees not too long, except for the thorny varieties. In March sow the grass seeds, plant out the little nasturtiums, keep a close eye on the gloxinia, orchids etc, in the greenhouse, as well as the plants under frames. Trim the borders as arranged; put wires in for the clematis and climbing roses as soon as Picard has done the necessary.

CLAUDE MONET, *Notes to his gardener, Giverny, 1900*

$\mathcal{I}$ think for wonderous variety, for certain picturesque qualities, for color and form and a subtle mystery of character, Poppies seem, on the whole, the most satisfactory flowers among the annuals. There is absolutely no limit to their variety of color. . . . To tell all the combinations of their wonderful hues, or even half, would be quite impossible, from the simple transparent scarlet bell of the wild Poppy to the marvelous pure white, the wonder of which no tongue can tell.

CELIA THAXTER, *An Island Garden*

JAPAN IN SPRING

All countries are beautiful in
Spring, but Japan is pre-eminently
so. The trees are now clothed with
leaves of the freshest green, and
many of the early flowering kinds
were in full blossom. On every hillside and in every cottage-garden
there was some object of attraction.
The double-blossomed cherry trees
and flowering peaches were most
beautiful objects, loaded as they now
were with flowers as large as little
roses.

ROBERT FORTUNE

Visits to the Capitals of Japan and China

*O*n this June day the buds in my garden are almost as enchanting as the open flowers. Things in bud bring, in the heat of a June noontide, the recollection of the loveliest days of the year—those days of May when all is suggested, nothing yet fulfilled.

MRS. FRANCIS KING

I am a flower gardener, and not a mere spreader about of bad carpets done in reluctant flowers, and when I had a garden of my own to make, I meant it to contain the greatest number of my favourite plants in the simplest way. . . .

WILLIAM ROBINSON

The Wild Garden

One of the daintiest joys of spring is the falling of soft rain among blossoms. The shining and apparently weightless drops come pattering into the maytree with a sound of soft laughter; one alights on a white petal with a little inaudible tap; then petal and raindrop fall together down the steeps of green and white, accompanied by troops of other petals, each with her attendant drop and her passing breath of scent.

MARY WEBB

$\mathcal{T}$o plant and maintain a flower-border, *with a good scheme for colour*, is by no means the easy thing that is commonly supposed.

I am strongly of the opinion that the possession of a quantity of plants, however good the plants may be themselves and however ample their number, does not make a garden; it only makes a *collection*. Having got the plants, the great thing is to use them with careful selection and definite intention. Merely having them, or having them planted unassorted in garden spaces, is only like having a box of paints from the best colourman, or, to go one step further, it is like having portions of these paints set out upon a palette.

GERTRUDE JEKYLL

Colour in the Flower Garden

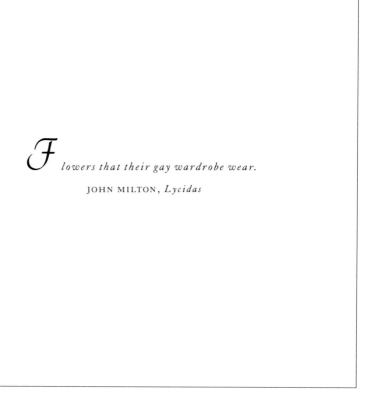

*F*lowers that their gay wardrobe wear.

JOHN MILTON, *Lycidas*

*T*he ideal of beauty is simplicity and tranquility.

JOHANN WOLFGANG VON GOETHE

*W*hen we first began to own a garden we could not bring ourselves to wait in patience for developments. We expected our beds to bloom as by magic. . . . But a garden is at once the most delightful and cunning of teachers. How kindly are the virtues it inculcates!—Patience, faith, hope, tenderness, gratitude, resignation, things in themselves as fragrant and beautiful as the flowers, or like the herbs, a little repellent of aspect, but sweet in their bruised savour.

AGNES AND EGERTON CASTLE

*F*ragrance, per-
haps, speaks more clearly, however,
to age than to youth. With the young
it may not pass much beyond the ol-
factory nerve, but with those who
have started down the far side of the
hill it reaches into the heart. . . . The
gardens of my youth were fragrant
gardens and it is their sweetness
rather than their patterns or their
furnishings that I now most clearly
recall.

LOUISE BEEBE WILDER
The Fragrant Path

*M*arian had not always been a great gardener. She had acquired the taste, with others, upon her second marriage. As mistress of the well laid out Martin "pleasure grounds," she had never thought of admitting a close acquaintance with her garden. That was the affair of the hirelings who tended it. At Lyndon, however, she realized that every lady in the country is a great gardener. The country dames who now called on her inquired tenderly after her herbaceous borders. They made nothing of asking each other for a root of this or that, which was apparently by way of being a compliment, though Marian thought it a very odd habit. She was a woman who could conform rapidly to any type, so she promptly provided herself with a large straw hat, leather gloves, and a pair of scissors. She took to spending her afternoons among the roses and learnt to talk of daphne cneorum, romneya, hepatica, arneria, gaultheria and berberis darwiniae. She flung a few of these exotic names about the drawing room now, and Agatha, duly impressed, wondered whether she, too, would be transmuted into a great gardener when she was established at Lyndon.

MARGARET KENNEDY, *The Ladies of Lyndon*

The kiss of the sun for pardon,

The song of the birds for mirth;

One is nearer God's Heart in a garden

Than anywhere else on earth.

DOROTHY FRANCES GURNEY
God's Garden

SOME EVENING SCENTED PLANTS

Acacia pendula

Allamanda cathartica 'Williamsii'

Bouvardia longiflora

Brassavola nodosa

Brugmansia suaveolens

Brunfelsia jamaicensis

Brunfelsia nitida

Cestrum aurantiacum

Cestrum nocturnum

Cestrum parqui

Daphne laureola

Daphne pontica

Datura spp.

Echinopsis multiplex

Epiphyllum oxypetalum

Gladiolus tristis

Hemerocallis flava

Hesperis matronalis

Hesperis tristis

Hoya bella

Hoya carnosa

Hoya lacunosa

Hylocereus undatus

Hymenocallis speciosa

Ipomoea alba

Jasminum sambac

Lilium spp.

Mahonia lomariifolia

Matthiola bicornis

Murraya exotica

Nicotiana alata

Nicotiana suaveolens

Nicotiana sylvestris

Oenothera biennis

Oenothera caespitosa

Pelargonium gibbosum

Polianthes tuberosa

Rondeletia odorata

Selenicereus grandiflorus

Trachelospermum asiaticum

Tropaeolum majus

Viola cornuta

I am quite of the opinion that a garden should look as though it belonged to a house, and the house as though it were conscious of and approved the garden. In passing from one to the other, one should experience no sense of discord, but the sensations produced by the one should be continued, with a delicate difference, by the other.

ALFRED AUSTIN

$\mathcal{T}$he formal treatment of gardens ought, perhaps, to be called the architectural treatment of gardens, for it consists in the extension of the principles of design which govern the house to the grounds which surround it. . . . Architecture in any shape has certain definite characteristics which it cannot get rid of; but, on the other hand, you can lay out the grounds, and alter the levels, and plant hedges and trees exactly as you please; in a word, you can so control and modify the grounds as to bring nature into harmony with the house, if you cannot bring the house into harmony with nature.

SIR REGINALD BLOMFIELD, *The Formal Garden in England*

Fresh spring the herald of love's mighty king,

In whose coat armour richly are display'd

All sorts of flowers the which on earth do spring

In goodly colours gloriously array'd

EDMUND SPENSER, *Amoretti*

48

*F*lowers of all heavens, and lovelier than their names.

ALFRED, LORD TENNYSON, *The Princess*

I have loved flowers that fade,

Within whose magic tents

Rich hues have marriage made

With sweet unmemoried scents.

ROBERT BRIDGES
I Have Loved Flowers That Fade

Go little book, and wish to all

Flowers in the garden, meat in the hall,

A bin of wine, spice of wit,

A house with lawns enclosing it,

A living river by the door,

A nightingale in the sycamore!

ROBERT LOUIS STEVENSON

Underwoods

"Book learning" gave me information, but only physical contact can give any real knowledge and understanding of a live organism. To have "green fingers" or a "green thumb" is an old expression which describes the art of communicating the subtle energies of love to prosper a living plant. . . . If you wish to make anything grow you must understand it, and understand it in a very real sense. "Green fingers" are a fact, and a mystery only to the unpractised. But green fingers are the extensions of a verdant heart. A good garden cannot be made by somebody who has not developed the capacity to know and to love growing things.

RUSSELL PAGE, *The Education of a Gardener*

*T*he Italian country house, especially in the center and south of Italy, was almost always built on a hillside, and one day the architect looked forth from the terrace of his villa, and saw that, in his survey of the garden, the enclosing landscape was naturally included: the two formed a part of the same composition. . . . The inherent beauty of the garden lies in the grouping of its parts—in the converging lines of its long ilex-walks, the alternation of sunny open spaces with cool woodland

shade, the proportion between terrace and bowling-green, or between the height of a wall and the width of a path. None of these details was negligible to the landscape-architect of the Renaissance: He considered the distribution of shade and sunlight, of straight lines of masonry and rippled lines of foliage, as carefully as he weighed the relation of his whole composition to the scene about it.

EDITH WHARTON
Italian Formality

T hen we pitched the sodden tents, and having lit a fire made some tea. There was ample time before dusk to climb the steep rock stairway which led towards the upper valley and the pass; and with my rucksack on my back I started off. A thin mist, gelid with half-frozen moisture, was driving gustily over the ridge, and every now and then a shower of rain swooped down, blotting out the mountains and chilling me to the bone. Between the showers, the pale winding-sheet of the mountain gleamed bleakly.

But if the weather was discomfiting, the scene which revealed itself to me as soon as I had ascended the first flight of rocks, compensated for every inconvenience. I was breathless, not merely with the ascent: the valley was alight with flowers! Rhododendrons, dwarf in stature, yet hoary with age, sprawled and writhed in every direction. I trod them underfoot, priceless blooms which many men have yearned to see. You could not walk without crushing them, the whole rock floor was hotly carpeted, and over the cliffs poured an incandescent stream of living lava.

F. KINGDON WARD, *The Romance of Gardening*

I shall be a gen'l'm'n myself one of
these days, perhaps, with a pipe in
my mouth, and a summer-house in
the back garden.

CHARLES DICKENS, *Pickwick Papers*

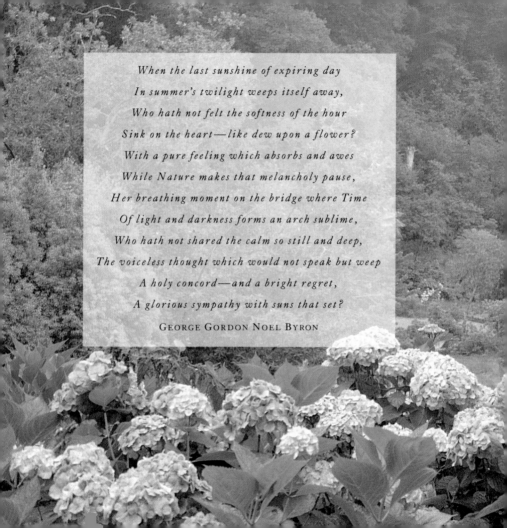

When the last sunshine of expiring day
In summer's twilight weeps itself away,
Who hath not felt the softness of the hour
Sink on the heart—like dew upon a flower?
With a pure feeling which absorbs and awes
While Nature makes that melancholy pause,
Her breathing moment on the bridge where Time
Of light and darkness forms an arch sublime,
Who hath not shared the calm so still and deep,
The voiceless thought which would not speak but weep
A holy concord—and a bright regret,
A glorious sympathy with suns that set?

GEORGE GORDON NOEL BYRON

*A*nd after all the weather was ideal. They could not have had a more perfect day for a garden-party if they had ordered it. Windless, warm, the sky without a cloud. Only the blue was veiled with a haze of light gold, as it is sometimes in early summer. The gardener had been up since dawn, mowing the lawns and sweeping them, until the grass and the dark flat rosettes

where the daisy plants had been seemed to
shine. As for the roses, you could not help
feeling they understood that roses are the only
flowers that impress people at garden parties;
the only flowers that everyone is certain of
knowing. Hundreds, yes, literally hundreds, had come out in a single night; the
green bushes bowed down as though they had
been visited by archangels.

KATHERINE MANSFIELD, *The Garden Party*

FLOWERS

. . . have a mysterious and subtle influence
upon the feelings, not unlike some strains
of music. They relax the tenseness of the
mind. They dissolve its rigor.

HENRY WARD BEECHER, *Eyes and Ears*

January	*Snow Month*
February	*Rain Month*
March	*Wind Month*
April	*Bud Month*
May	*Flower Month*
June	*Heat Month*

July	Hay Month
August	Harvest Month
September	Fruit Month
October	Grape Month
November	Fog Month
December	Winter Month

FROM AN OLD QUAKER CALENDAR

*T*he love of flowers is really the best teacher
of how to grow and understand them.

MAX SCHLING
Everyman's Garden

*W*ater . . . is the most interesting object in a landscape, and the happiest circumstance in a retired recess; captivates the eye at a distance, invites approach, and is delightful when near; it refreshes an open exposure; it animates a shade; cheers the dreariness of a waste, and enriches the most crowded view: in form, in style, and in extent, may be made equal to the greatest compositions, or adapted to the least: It may spread in a calm expanse to sooth the tranquility of a peaceful scene; or hurrying along a devious course, add splendor to a gay, and extravagance to a romantic, situation.

THOMAS WHATELY, *Observations on Modern Gardening*

*N*ow is
the time of the illumi-
nated woods . . . every
leaf glows like a tiny
lamp; one walks
through their lighted
halls with a curious
enjoyment.

JOHN BURROUGHS

*The Heart of
Burroughs' Journals*

*I*t was a morning of ground mist, yellow sunshine, and high rifts of blue, white-cloud-dappled sky. The leaves were still thick on the trees, but dew-spangled gossamer threads hung on the bushes and the shrill little cries of unrest of the swallows skimming the green open spaces of the park told of autumn and change.

FLORA THOMPSON, *Lark Rise to Candleford*

*A*s is the garden such is the gardener.
A man's nature runs either to herbs or weeds.

FRANCIS BACON

ast night, there came a frost, which has done great damage to my garden. . . . It is sad that Nature will play such tricks with us poor mortals, inviting us with sunny smiles to confide in her, and then, when we are entirely within her power, striking us to the heart.

NATHANIEL HAWTHORNE, *The American Notebooks*

Hours fly

Flowers die.

New days,

New ways

Pass by;

Love stays.

REV. HENRY VAN DYKE

While we slept, these formal gardens
Worked into their disguise. The Warden's
Judas and tulip trees awake

In ermine. Here and there a flake
Of white falls from the painted scene,
Or a dark scowl of evergreen
Glares through the shroud, or a leaf dumps
Its load and the soft burden slumps
Earthward like a fainting girl.

CECIL DAY LEWIS

I have often thought that if heaven had given me choice of
my position and calling, it should have been on a rich
spot of earth, well watered, and near a good market for
the productions of the garden. No occupation is so delightful to me as the culture of the earth, and no culture
comparable to that of the garden. Such a variety of sub-
jects, some one always coming to perfection, the failure
of one thing repaired by the success of another, and in-
stead of one harvest a continued one through the year.
Under a total want of demand except for our family table,
I am still devoted to the garden. But though an old man,
I am but a young gardener.

THOMAS JEFFERSON

GARDENS OF CHILDHOOD

There is a garden in every childhood, an enchanted place where colors are brighter, the air softer, and the morning more fragrant than ever again.

ELIZABETH LAWRENCE

A Southern Garden

BIOGRAPHIES

Alfred Austin (1835–1913), English author

Francis Bacon (1561–1626), English philosopher, essayist, and statesman

Henry Ward Beecher (1813–1887), American Congregational preacher and lecturer

Sir Reginald Blomfield (1856–1942), English architect and author

John Burroughs (1837–1921), American naturalist and author

George Gordon Noel Byron (1788–1824), English poet and satirist

Charles Dickens (1812–1870), English novelist

Robert Fortune (1813–1880), English botanist and plant hunter

Johann Wolfgang von Goëthe (1749–1832), German poet, dramatist, and novelist

Nathaniel Hawthorne (1804–1864), American novelist and short-story writer

Thomas Jefferson (1743–1826), third President of the United States

Gertrude Jekyll (1843–1932), English garden designer

Margaret Kennedy (1896–1967), English novelist and playwright

Mrs. Francis King (1864–1948), garden writer, a founder of Garden Club of America

F. Kingdon-Ward (1885–1958), plant collector, geographer, and author

Elizabeth Lawrence (1910–1985), English garden writer and novelist

Cecil Day Lewis (1904–1972), English author and poet

Katherine Mansfield (1910–1985), New Zealand-born short-story writer, poet, and critic

Claude Monet (1840–1926), French landscape painter, a founder of Impressionism

Russell Page (1906–1985), English landscape architect

William Robinson (1838–1935), Irish gardener and writer

William Shakespeare (1564–1616), English dramatist and poet

Edmund Spenser (1552–1599), English poet, author of *The Faerie Queene*

Robert Louis Stevenson (1850–1894), Scottish novelist, poet, and essayist

Celia Thaxter (1835–1894), American poet and garden writer

Flora Thompson (1877–1947), English novelist and poet

Henry van Dyke (1852–1933), American clergyman, educator, and author

Mary Webb (1881–1927), English novelist

Edith Wharton (1862–1937), American novelist

Thomas Whately (d. 1772), English politician and garden designer

Louise Beebe Wilder (1878–1938), American garden writer

ACKNOWLEDGMENTS

Excerpt from *The Ladies of Lyndon* by
Margaret Kennedy. Reprinted by permission of Virago Press.

Excerpt from *A Southern Garden* by
Elizabeth Lawrence. Copyright
© 1942, 1967, 1984 by The University
of North Carolina Press. Used by
permission.

"Snowfall on a College Garden" by
Cecil Day Lewis. Copyright the estate
of C. Day Lewis and used by
permission.

Excerpt from "The Garden Party" by
Katherine Mansfield from *The Collected
Works of Katherine Mansfield*. Copyright
© 1922 by Alfred A. Knopf, renewed
1950 by John Middleton Murry. Reprinted by permission of Alfred A.
Knopf.

Excerpt from *Education of a Gardener*
by Russell Page. Copyright © 1985 by
Random House. Reprinted by permission of Random House, Inc.

"The Garden" by R. S. Thomas from
Poems of R. S. Thomas. Copyright
© 1983 by the University of Arkansas
Press. Reprinted by permission of the
University of Arkansas Press.

Excerpt from *Poems and Spring of Joy* by
Mary Webb. Reprinted by permission
of Jonathan Cape Publishers.

ART CREDITS

Boys Syndication/Jacqui Hurst: 22,
32–33, 35, 47, 66–67, 86–87, 96;
Richard W. Brown: 20–21, 27, 90;
Karen Bussolini: Jacket background;
Country Life: 29; E T Archive: 63;
Garden Picture Library: Jacket front,
1, 6, 12–13, 15, 16, 18–19, 25, 31,
40–41, 44, 51 (top and bottom), 55, 56,
58–59, 60–61, 71, 80–81, 82–83, 85;
Rob Gray: 65; Andrew Lawson: 10–11,
79, 88, 89; Jerry Pavia: 76, 92–93;
Royal Commission on Historical
Monuments: 74; Lauren Springer: 37,
39, 49, 53.